LOOKING INTO

# SOIL

BY EMMA HUDDLESTON

**The Child's World®**
childsworld.com

Published by The Child's World®
1980 Lookout Drive • Mankato, MN 56003-1705
800-599-READ • www.childsworld.com

Photographs ©: Mr. Rawin Tanpin/Shutterstock Images, cover (background), 1 (background), 2 (background); Shutterstock Images, cover (root), 1 (root), 16; Bob Pool/Shutterstock Images, cover (pill bug), 1 (pill bug), 2 (pill bug), 21; Picture Partners/Shutterstock Images, cover (worm), 1 (worm), 24; iStockphoto, 5, 12, 17; Daniel Lacy/iStockphoto, 6; Vasiliy Budarin/iStockphoto, 9; Connie Kerr/iStockphoto, 10; Chantale Ouellet/iStockphoto, 13; V. Sanandhakrishna/iStockphoto, 14; Rita Meraki/Shutterstock Images, 18

ISBN 9781503835207
LCCN 2019943115

Printed in the United States of America

## ABOUT THE AUTHOR

Emma Huddleston is a children's book author. She lives in Minnesota with her husband. She enjoys learning about the world in which we live while she writes.

# TABLE OF CONTENTS

# CHAPTER ONE

# What Is Soil?

**S**oil is different in all parts of the world. Dry, dusty soil lies in deserts. Rain forests have damp, soggy soil. Soil is made of air, water, **minerals**, and **organic** matter packed together. Soil forms in layers. The main soil layers are topsoil, subsoil, and parent material. Some areas of the world have a top layer of **decaying** plants and other organic matter. Soil can also have a sandy layer. Sometimes soil sits on top of solid rock, called bedrock.

Some areas of the world have more soil than others. Soil ranges from a few inches to several feet thick. Different areas can also have different layers. Soil's features depend on the soil's surroundings and how the soil formed.

# Layers of Soil

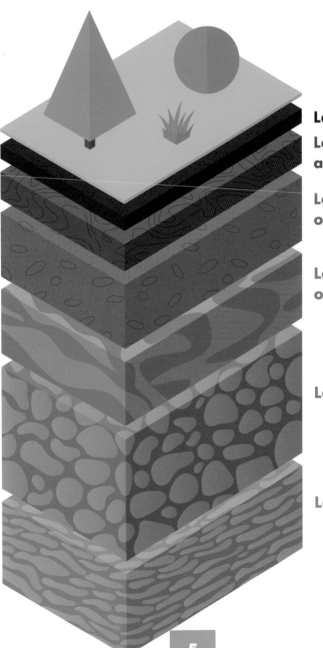

**Organic Layer**

**Layer of decaying organic matter**

Layer with most organic matter and activity

**Topsoil**

**Sandy Layer**

Layer missing minerals and organic matter

**Subsoil**

Layer rich in minerals with some organic matter

**Parent Material**

Layer of partly weathered rock

Layer of solid rock

**Bedrock**

When plants break up rocks, it is called organic weathering.

Soil forms as rocks are slowly worn down by weathering. Sunlight, air, water, and living things cause weathering. Sunlight dries rocks. Dry rocks crumble over time. Wind blows small pieces loose. Rainwater fills tiny holes in rocks. The water freezes and expands. The frozen water cracks the rock. Plants dig their roots into the cracks. The roots break apart the rocks. People and animals walk all over the ground. They push down and kick away the earth beneath them. Little by little, all these broken materials stack up. They mix together with organic matter. This forms soil. Some areas of soil have formed over thousands of years. Others have formed over hundreds of years. Soil is always changing and always forming.

# CHAPTER TWO

# Topsoil

Topsoil is often the top layer of soil. It is a mix of minerals and organic matter. Organic matter includes things that are living or were once living. Less than 15 percent of soil's organic matter is living. The living parts of soil include bacteria, plant roots, and insects.

Sometimes there is an organic layer above the topsoil. The organic layer is mostly made of dead plants and leaves. Eventually the organic matter breaks down. It forms **humus** (HYOO-muss). Humus is thick and dark. It is created from very decayed matter.

Humus can be dark brown or black.

Fungi help organic matter decay.

Decay is a natural process of breaking down. For example, animal waste drops to the ground. Fallen leaves and dead plants create litter piles. Bodies of dead insects and animals add to the piles. As these things decay, their **nutrients** return to the soil. Living things use these nutrients. Humus is a part of healthy soil. It holds many nutrients. It also helps soil crumble. This lets water and air move easily through it. Then the water and air can reach plant roots.

Worms' holes help water and plant roots get deep into the soil.

The topsoil is where most activity takes place in soil. Creatures such as worms live there. They crawl around and mix humus from the organic layer into the topsoil. They also help break down waste. Plants grow roots into topsoil. They take in water and nutrients from it. The plants become food for animals and humans. Some animals also dig into soil for shelter. Chipmunks dig holes up to 3 inches (8 cm) wide. They hide in the soil from larger animals.

Chipmunks store food for the winter in their holes.

Clay has been used to create things such as bricks and pottery for thousands of years.

# CHAPTER THREE

# Subsoil

Beneath topsoil is subsoil. Subsoil has less organic matter than topsoil. It has less humus. With little humus, subsoil has a light color. Subsoil is mostly made of minerals. These minerals are important for plant growth. Plant roots grow down into the subsoil. There, they take in minerals.

Clay is common in subsoil. Clay is a type of soil. It is hard when dry and sticky when wet. It is made of very fine, tiny pieces. They are packed tightly together. Some clay in soil forms blocks. Clay can also form columns.

## Soil Sciences

**Pedology** and **edaphology** are soil sciences. Pedology studies different types of soil and compares them. It looks at soil and its surroundings. It studies soil layers. Edaphology studies how soil forms. It looks at the ways soil affects living things. Edaphology also studies how people use soil.

The minerals and organic matter in subsoil came from the soil above. They were pulled down through a process called **leaching**. Water on the surface of the soil moves downward through the soil. As water seeps down, it dissolves minerals. It can also move pieces of rock, soil, and organic matter. It pulls these things down with it. They gather in the subsoil.

Sometimes there is a sandy layer between topsoil and subsoil. This layer has lost most of its minerals and organic matter. Water leaches the minerals and organic matter out of it. The water leaves behind a layer of mostly sand.

The sandy layer often occurs in forests.

SANDY LAYER

The United States has more than 20,000 different types of soil.

# CHAPTER FOUR

# Parent Material

**B**eneath subsoil is parent material. Parent material is made of mineral and organic matter that has been partly weathered. It is where soil comes from. The type of parent material affects the features of the soil above it. Not all rocks are the same. So when they are weathered, they create different types of soil. Soil that is close to the parent material shares more features with it.

Soil can have different colors. The soil can be fine or coarse. Fine soil is made of tiny pieces. These pieces can pack tightly together. This creates a firm layer. Coarse soil is made of larger pieces. It is more difficult to pack together. It forms weak layers.

Sometimes parent material sits above bedrock. Bedrock is a solid layer of rock beneath soil. Water, wind, and other natural forces can move the soil and uncover bedrock. Uncovered bedrock is called an outcrop. Outcrops occur naturally on mountaintops and rocky coasts. As outcrops are weathered, the bedrock becomes parent material. As the parent material is weathered, soil builds up on top of it. The pile of matter on the parent material gets thicker and thicker. Eventually, soil's layers form.

Most living things depend on soil. It holds important nutrients. It helps plants grow. Plants become food for animals and people. People create things using soil and build on top of it. Soil connects and supports life on Earth.

# FAST FACTS

- Soil is made of air, water, minerals, and organic matter.

- Weathering forms soil.

- Topsoil is rich in humus and nutrients.

- Topsoil is where most activity takes place in soil.

- Subsoil is mostly made of minerals.

- Minerals and organic matter leach into subsoil.

- Soil forms from parent material.

- Bedrock is weathered into parent material.

# INDEX